In *How to See the World,* Paula J. Lambert takes us deftly along as she examines the new reality in which we've all awakened in 2020. She peels back its complicated layers with adept use of metaphor, as well as a revelatory tone that will have readers doubling back to unfold new meanings in a line, a verse, or a poem. Real moments of brilliance sparkle and call us to look beyond surface and pattern to recognize something beyond ourselves, even while we languish in a groundswell of change.

*Tell me moonlight can't speak...*she writes, then convinces us that it can. While pandemic exists and is unavoidable, do not approach this collection as an outgassing of that reality. It is about much more: how interconnected we all are while teetering at the brink of change and that we must witness life's miracle, and not turn away.

—Rose M. Smith, author of *Unearthing Ida*

OTHER WORKS BY PAULA J. LAMBERT

Hyacinth: Poems of the Spring Pandemic (Self-published, 2020)
A Lesson in Possibilities (Self-published with support from the Greater Columbus Arts Council, 2019)
The Ecstasy of Wanting (Full/Crescent Press 2018)
The Sudden Seduction of Gravity (Full/Crescent Press 2012).
The Guilt That Gathers (Pudding House Press 2009)

HARMONY SERIES

BOTTOM DOG PRESS

How to See the World

Paula J. Lambert

Harmony Series
Bottom Dog Press
Huron, Ohio 44839

ISBN: 978-1-947504-23-3
Bottom Dog Press, Inc.
PO Box 425, Huron, OH 44839
Lsmithdog@aol.com
http://smithdocs.net

CREDITS:
General Editor: Larry Smith
Layout Design and Cover Layout: Susanna Sharp-Schwacke
Cover Image: Paula J. Lambert
Cover Consultant: Ali Wade

ACKNOWLEDGEMENTS:

The following poems were published (some in slightly different form) in the benefit chapbook *Hyacinth*, published by the author May 2020: "Breath"; "What Happens at the End of the Inhale"; "Off Course"; "Hyacinth"; "Opossum: Diversion, Strategy"; "Cloistered"; "Ant: Patience"; "The Breath You're Holding (Easter Prayer)"; "Wilt: Tulip Magnolia"; "The Detail Left Out"; "Unafraid"; "Scraps: Ritual, Rebirth"; "Earth Day Dream: Rumi".

The author is also grateful for the following:
"The Breath You're Holding" was included in a video produced by Healing Broken Circles for the Marion Correctional Institution. April 2020.
"Opossum: Diversion, Strategy" was shared on Episode #125, Open Mic of the Air #4, *Poetry Spoken Here*. Apple Podcast. May 1, 2020.
"Brave: Titan Arum" was shared on the Barnard College Arthur Ross Greenhouse Instagram page. May 29, 2020.
"Beast" and "Flying" were published in *Eunoia Review*, June 18, 2020.
"Justice" was published in *Eclipsing the Dark: The Sun & Moon Poetry Festival 2014-2019* (OPA Press, 2020).
"How to See the World: Hunger," "How to See the World: Thirst," and "How to See the World: Fire" were published in *Flights 2020*.

Table of Contents

III.

IV.

For Elizabeth

If you notice anything,
It leads you to notice
more
and more.

—Mary Oliver

Look, and look again.

—Mary Oliver

I.

Fruit

I learned I was supposed to clean my groceries on the same day
the hurt began, the missing-so-much-it-hurt, but I was still trying
to ignore that a while longer. And, here they were, the groceries,

piled on the floor in a room we just don't use anymore. God
knows how many hands have touched it: shipping to shelves to
checkout to here. The man on the video said to wipe the plastic

packaging, pull saltine sleeves from their tainted cardboard box,
wash your produce like you wash your hands. So I let fruit tumble
to the sink, each piece a soft splash of the sudsy water, oranges

first, big and round and bright as never you mind. I held one
in my hand, cradling it like my granddaughter's head, sweetly,
carefully, washing it like I might wash her cheeks, *don't you cry,*

sweetheart, don't you cry. Was it her I whispered to or was it me,
dipping the perfect piece of fruit in the rinse and setting it softly
on the counter to wipe dry later. Funny how everything I do

now extends to something else, every touch, every thought, every
worry, each fond thought. Making love to my husband now like
sending love to the world: kisses blow past his cheek to the wind

outside, every moan, every sigh, a memory tied to every possible
part of my life. It's not theory anymore that we're all connected,
that everything is, and here, now, reaching for a lemon bouncing

through the suds, I hold it in my hand, think, *this was the size of her*
head when she was born, and so it was. I said so then only called it a
peach, fuzzy and pink: premature. I hold this lemon the way I held

her, tenderly, tearful, some combination of awe and love. How
bright is this tiny sweet lemon, how yellow, how lovely these tiny
dimpled pocks on its skin. I reach for each newly-cleansed orange,

each lemon, each honey-crisp apple, dry it with a soft cotton cloth
saying *don't you worry, now. Everything will be all right.* I let myself
believe that's true, piling fruit perfectly into green-glass bowls.

Breath

This is how the world has always lived: lonely
and afraid, each wave of terrible news an intake

of breath, sharp, a steel-bright sword to our side.
The long, slow, angry exhale prepares us for

what bitter thing comes next: sunrise, laughter,
rain. Crocus, wise and delicate, blooms through

death again and again. We can be that bursting.
This is how the earth has always lived. This is

what it is: earth cracks open, we reach for light.
Darkness comes, we reach for light once more.

What Happens at the End of the Inhale

Nothing, really. A pause, a lingering,
a glance toward the window. Outside,

magnolia blossoms, fattening all day,
have not yet burst. There's only this:

a deepening color, a slow unfolding,
the soothing reminder to let things go.

Every Wednesday at Noon

The tornado siren sounds. Not a warning,
no imminent threat: this is a test. And if

this were any old Wednesday, you might
think *hmph, 12:00 already* and move on

with your day. But these are not normal
times as we're reminded by every single

ad on every single device we own. *In these*
unprecedented times... Your heart stops,

briefly, body floods with adrenalin, brain
says, WHAT NOW MY GOD WHAT NOW

before shifting back to silence. I'm not kidding
when I say I was made for these times. I've

prepared my entire life. I know these sirens
well, these false starts, this frozen in place,

the *breathejustpleasebreathe* response. My
heart has run a million miles: it takes more

than this to stop it. I've seen what happens
when the sirens are real, the aftermath. I know

when to play it safe, how to go underground.
How the heart calms itself. How breath returns.

Respite

We're going to do it as soon as possible. So
it can be useful...and that it remains forever.
—Nadia Calviño

A warm day in spring, full of sun, clears
the mind. Respite from the blitz of rain

and wind and cold I know is still bound
to muscle its way back through. In short:

it's been a good day, but I know the forecast
for tomorrow. Earlier, I woke with a start

from the sound of my own snore and saw
the new headline: Spain Announces UBI.

And Rebecca Solnit said: *Disasters often*
unfold like revolutions. Ain't it the truth.

And so my day ends how it began, with
a glimmer of hope. *And yeah*, says Solnit,

counterrevolution is also part of the package. So
it goes. One poem opens itself into two

new threads then knits itself back: Hope
followed by storms of uncertainty followed

by new hope followed again by...well. What
wants to kill us won't die. But by god neither

will we. Even in the midst of all this, I believe
in what's good, what's fair, what's right.

Hyacinth

Walking down the center of the street,
keeping a wide berth from...everything,
I marveled at how many more flowers

were blooming than I'd realized, yellow
and white, daffodils mainly, set against
the greenest grass I'd ever witnessed.

The dog I saw ahead was tied to a stake
that looked strong enough to hold him,
so I wished even him well this evening.

We eyed each other quietly, and I felt his
sorrow: red fawn boxer, yellow cord,
off-white stake. He, too, contained in a

way he wasn't built for. He barked once.
I know, I told him. *I feel it too, old friend.*
He couldn't bear the sympathy, barked

again, strained against the cord, and for
the first time, I doubted we were made
for these times. Turning the corner, I saw

pink and purple in the yard across the
street: hyacinth. I made my way toward
them, refusing to let my heart be broken.

Cloistered

My son in New York City says the sirens never
stop. He's heard as many as five at once. Here

in the suburbs of central Ohio they're still few
and far between. It's the lawnmowers that never

end; we've not yet learned to let our grass grow
wild. I lay on my back on my sun-drenched deck

marveling at how long it's taken me to ask how to
love my neighbors when I do not always like them.

One mower stops and another, further away, still
roars. It stops, and I can hear another. It's a gradual

lessening. I count the continual distant hum all
the way back to Brooklyn. I've not yet told

Christopher about my cousin in Queens. Instead,
I let these squawking birds pull me back to where

I am right now: cloistered paradise. Christopher is
a variant of Christ. (Aren't we all?) My great aunts,

cloistered nuns, must have had bad days. Sad days.
Abbey monks making all those sweet preserves

must have pissed each other off plenty. We cultivate
silence, I see so much better now: it's the chance

to trace all we feel to its source, forward and back
through every generation across space and time.

And this squawking jay, thinking I'm too close,
was sent to calm my monkey mind. *There are better*

things to do, he says, *than to dwell anyplace but here.*

Opossum: Diversion, Strategy

Yesterday, a friend found a opossum dead
in her garage. Dead-dead. Once she collected
herself, she buried it. Faithful girl. We deal

with what we must. Opossum tells us to let
the ego go, rely on instinct, prepare for the
unexpected. Use the brain as a tool to survive.

When the enemy thinks we're dead, we collect
ourselves and move to safety. Smart opossum.
Wise opossum. Contrary, dead opossum tells

us this: drama doesn't help. You're not really
a victim. All we need is to buy ourselves some
time. Anyway, that's what my friend's opossum

said to me. It's what the burial played out:
do what you must. Respect the ritual. When
this threat, too, has passed, we all move on.

Off Course

This morning, a hooded oriole arrived
in Ohio and settled into a blossoming
cherry tree. Strange and beautiful, this

clashing: orange bird, black mask, wild
explosion of pink all around him. He, too,
is in seclusion. They're called vagrants,

these birds blown so far off course. They
rarely survive. Not long ago, a masked
booby rode a gulf-coast hurricane north,

landed in Cape Cod and died a few days
later. It's the young adults, so unused to
traveling at all, who tend to stray like this.

(Didn't we all, once? Didn't we hope to?)
But not all the accidentals die. Darwin's
finches bloomed like these pink blossoms.

Hawaiian honeycreepers sing all across
that strand of jeweled islands. We survive
all the ways that we can, spirits blown

off course. And when we don't, we ride
currents of air that caress us all, winds
whispering: *Don't you worry, loves. Don't*

you worry. We've all been blown off course:
it doesn't mean we're lost. Hear them now,
whispering? Spirits saying, *We're still here.*

Wilt: Tulip Magnolia

The blossoms have browned. What hasn't
already blown from the branches of this tree
wilts from its limbs, waiting to finally just

fall. The ground is saturated with rain. Grass,
swamped by its own saving, sees what's
budding above: green leaves waking, waiting

to stretch and yawn in the sun. Grass grows
higher. Limbs bend lower. This happens every
year, I tell myself. This happens every year.

The Breath You're Holding

The man who invented the first reliable
mass-produced ventilator was named
Forrest Bird. I cried when I learned this.

My father, the first person I ever saw on
a vent, was also the first I ever saw die.
It would be wrong to say a Bird couldn't

save him. Once, walking in the woods,
he let loose his trademark whistle;
a mockingbird sang it straight back. My

father was transformed. I was witness to
the sound. I never saw the bird that day
but when I listen, I can always hear Dad.

It can't be coincidence that Forrest Bird
was an aviator, that he piloted planes
when they started to fly so high that

humans could no longer breathe. Bird
paid attention. He listened to his own calling.
Both these things are true: there are not

enough vents, there are not enough birds.
But when I stand in the forest and listen,
every song drifting back is my father and me,

every call is your dad and you; the wind
in the trees is the same as each cry that ever
leapt from our throats. So, let's try this:

breathe in deep and slow, lift your arms
out wide. Believe in a Bird that can
save us. Let the breath you're holding go.

Dead of Winter

Perhaps the Germans have a word for it
or maybe the Japanese. Something long
and lovely and untranslatable: waiting for

those who died in winter to be put to rest
in the spring. There's nuance, I'm sure, in
knowing it's regional, that it happens only

up north. I remember this: ice fishing with
my grandfather. Chiseling a hole, dropping
the line, trusting that something would

bite. (At what point in our human evolution
did we come to believe that only the surface
was frozen?) Soil is solid in winter. Nothing

waits underneath—or at least, you can't set
a line for what's there. So we wait for spring
to plant our seedlings, to put our bodies to

rest. What is the word, again, for this feeling?
And which country is it that knows what
to call it when spring comes but the waiting

goes on? Tell me the language they use for
seeds sprouting into terrible beauty while
grief knows it's only the longing that grows.

Scraps: Ritual, Rebirth

It took a week to arrive, these groceries. Oh,
what nurtures! Oh, what we consume! I save
what I once tossed away: base of the celery,

bottom of this onion bulb. I float them in water,
set the glass in the sun. What's left is only my
own agnosticism: will there be a resurrection?

The celery sits, the roots of the onion swell.
Already this mirrors what I've come to know:
first, the deep dive, that blind wanting. What

doesn't know yet if it wants to go on. Time
and sunlight, darkness and sun again. Then
the tiniest, tiniest glimmer of sprout. I lean in.

Celery is sprouting, I'm sure of it now. And
at the center of its loosely layered rings, onion
is birthing. I consider the ritual of death and

rebirth, how these still-reaching roots will return
to the soil. I think what they might suffer: deer,
rabbit, raccoon. I think how they might grow.

I think about hunger, humbling itself, think how
the scraps of what once fed us, nurtured and
transformed, lead back to what feeds us again.

Washing

dishes in the kitchen sink, the big
bowls, (so much baking lately, so

much making) and seeing how one
bowl slides so easily into the next,

I think *another revelation!* How easy
this is. How easily connection is

made when we're allowed to listen
to our own rhythms! And it almost

begins to assuage my terrible guilt
for not wanting this to end…

Unafraid

Yesterday I felt myself
levitate,
watched from the couch
as it happened. There I was,
suspended in the corner,
floating
over the flatscreen TV.
I wished I'd known beforehand
this could happen: revelation

comes when we least
expect it. Like when Dave died,
and it was so sudden and awful.
There he was
sitting next to me saying,
It's okay,
I'm okay.
As soon as I believed him,
he disappeared.

I watched myself quite a while
yesterday, unafraid.
I wake now wondering if
I'm still there.

II.

Tag

The game starts with eeny, meeny,
miny, moe and no one wants to be
It. But It chases us all till we're out

and the last one standing starts the
next round: on it goes. London Bridge
was always falling down. Red Rover

Red Rover was my personal terror,
ever the weak link in that wall. We
believed Ring Around the Rosies

was reference to the plague. It wasn't.
What garish belief was that, after
two world wars? The point is this:

kids continue to play after disasters
real and imagined. Grown folk give
meaning to their own delusions. That

doesn't stop the sing-song rhyming.
My fair lady, pocket full of posies.
Ashes ashes, duck duck goose. Miss

Mary Mack Mack Mack all dressed
in black black black. Tag. Tag. Tag.
You're it.

Closing In

Some mornings I swear I can hear it: the voice of John-Boy
Walton now grown saying *Spring went on and on that year*

while the camera pans across the mountain. *Earth bloomed
and the sky clouded over, releasing one more snow.* Eventually,

the camera closed in on Ike's General Store or Pa's sawmill,
and there'd be John-Boy arguing again with Mary Ellen,

Grandma pushing through the screen door that knocks closed
behind her (grumpy again, but by the end of the show with

that light in her eyes, shooing Grandpa back in with a cloth
napkin pulled from the clothesline: *You old fool!* You know

what always follows that: *Good night, John-Boy! Good night,
Mary Ellen! Good night, Grandma! Good night, Grandpa!* and

we'd be back to the voice of grown-man John-Boy summing
things up: *Summer did finally come to the mountain that year.*

*The war ended, and Ma came out of that bed no longer stricken
with polio.* And you knew whatever it was that had plagued

the mountain, the Waltons moved on. You'd go to bed, and
you'd sleep well, believing the mountain was still there.

ANSWER TO PRAYER

I don't remember the dream I had last night,
but know it centered on my mother. And it
was comforting. It was a little like those videos

now going around: every episode of *Friends*
played at once—though that was mostly just
a layer of tense whispering—or the triple layer

mash-up of "Somebody That I Used to Know."
I dreamt of every smile that ever graced her
face, every tender touch of her hand on mine.

It was the first time, maybe, that I woke up
rested and assured. Even this could be traced
to a meme: "I am asking people who LOVE

their Mom to join the challenge of posting
a photo. One photo only of your MOM." Just
like me, really, and like her, to amp things up

into overdrive. Get it done and move on:
you've always been loved. My mother was
tender in ways I haven't always given her

credit for. She's insistent now, in the dream,
that it was ever so, the layers assurance of
what I believe: we've many mothers, holy

and alive and tender with grace. Mother Mary,
Mother Earth, the Moon. Each has been as
tender as I dreamed. Each an answer to prayer.

Digging a Hole to China

Scrolling through what's trending
on Twitter, I see that *Tech Insider* is
asking if I ever tried to dig a hole

to China. Why, yes. Yes, I have.
With an old tin spoon in a patch
of dirt under the lilacs outside

my front door. *Tech Insider* tells me
it wouldn't have been possible, not
without hooking a wide left turn

since the other side of the world is
a spot somewhere in the middle of
the Indian Ocean. I guess they want

5-year-old me to know that when I
came up out of that hole I'd drown,
as if an obstacle as big as an ocean

was ever enough to stop a child
from dreaming, a child who knew
she could drag a boat behind her,

a child who could hold her breath
while her dad counted to ten, to
twenty-five, a hundred, a thousand.

The same dad who gave her that
spoon, who said China was a country
far away, a place past the ants she'd

find, all the scrapes on her fingers,
past the fire in the center of the earth,
a place on the other side of everything.

CHRISTMAS

My husband tells me about being a boy in Georgia,
about Christmas eve, about bundling in the car to
visit all the grandparents and cousins in the country.

He tells me the food was so plentiful on the farm that
scraps were fed to the dogs (which explains a lot about
my husband and leftovers). He tells me how every year

his dad brought cigarettes and handkerchiefs for
the men—he can't remember what his mom brought
for the women—but every year was exactly the same

and the best part, always, was the Piper Cub airplane
that flew over the field, someone shouting *Merrrrry*
Christmas from a megaphone while parachutes tied to

stockings full of toys and candy rained right down
from the sky. One year, the best year, his grandparents
gave him a melodica. He sat in the yard all by himself,

till the Piper Cub came and even after, till his parents
packed up the car and brought them back home, still
he sat up with that melodica all alone teaching himself

"Silent Night" from the little book that came in the box.
Come Christmas morning, he played the song for his
family. It's such a nice story. I've heard it all before.

But he tells it now with a wistfulness I'm not sure I've
heard from him ever, just after I tell him my cousin
Hilary posted on Facebook about her son playing his

melodica. I can't stop thinking about breath, that this
sweet silly instrument works with the breath, that when
my husband tells me his melodica memory every detail

is also, one way or another, about breath: cigarettes and
even those handkerchiefs, the magical airplane riding
on air, the parachutes floating down. And him, tiny boy

with the greatest gift he'd even been given: something
he can cast his breath through and plink his fingers
over so somewhere through a silent southern night,

music floats back up to where the Piper Cub was.
On Christmas morning in Clayton County, he played
the song he'd figured out on the farm. He tells me

about it now, sixty years later, on a walk through the
suburbs in Ohio, as committed an atheist as ever there
was. But there's no denying the light in his eyes, that

once upon a time, even he believed in something. Not
God, of course. Even at five or six years old, he claims,
he knew something wasn't right with that story. He

believed he could learn a tune, and he never would
have guessed he'd be telling me about it so many years
later, so many miles away, after my cousin posted on

Facebook, while we're all sheltering in place, while he
and I are walking through the neighborhood before
this storm blows in, one that's already blowing through

these trees. That's god for me, how breath can blow
"Silent Night" through sixty years of memory, connect
one part of family to another. Don't tell me every puff

of smoke his uncles blew didn't rise up, too, wherever
it was that Piper Cub came from. Don't tell me that
a melodica in New York City didn't just play in Ohio.

What would god be if not this breath, this music, this
breeze? What if not parachutes filled with Christmas
toys? What if not this sadness? What, if not this joy?

Blue

Was that it? you ask about the dream.
Or was there more? Kvetch, I say. That

one about the kvetching. You repeat
the word, roll it on your tongue like

soup: *kvetch*. I try to explain. It's not my
word. Dreams speak their own language.

There was a low, crusty murmur. In
the center, a soft, blue blanket. You

watch me, expecting more. Like that,
I say. Consternation, just like that.

Innocence in the face of it all. Waiting
for something you could understand.

My Front Door

It must have been practical once,
back when the house was built,

before the invention of cars. You
didn't need much that you couldn't

get to on foot: grocer, factory, post
office, school. This fancy front door

with the stained-glass panels that
barely let in any light has hardly

been opened in years. When it is,
it opens to Mill Street, which all by

itself alludes to the mills that were
open then too, and to people who

earned their living without boarding
the train into Boston. When I was

a kid, we came in through the back,
banged into and out of the house

through a door always testing its
hinges. The screened-in porch let

in flies and mosquitoes and bees
from the lilac bushes along with

the stingy breeze. That was back
when you spoke to your neighbors,

knew every one by name. The past
is past, Mom always said, hers so

different from ours, ours different
from whomever might live here

next. Will they know the ancestors
knocking around, Aunt Rose with

the broken hip? I saw her once when
I was twelve, my mom's great aunt,

waiting at the bottom of the stairs.
She came to be sure we knew who

she was, said no one who lives wants
to die, or once dead, to be forgotten.

Who would pass through even a bright
and beautiful door knowing they won't

be let back in? Doors are made to be
opened. Closed, they must open again.

TELL ME HOW WE MET. MAKE IT A LIE.

The truth is so uninteresting: we met at a party. My best friend
was dating your best friend. We became a foursome. Please,
tell me a lie. Or at least skip ahead. You were in college, I was
in art school, we met at the weekend film festival. We were

wearing pajamas, so there was no pressure later. We stayed there
overnight, two nights, so there was no pressure later. *Monty Python
and the Holy Grail* was your favorite movie. You laughed one beat
ahead of every joke in every scene, and it wasn't annoying.

Your eyes crinkled closed just before you threw your head back
to laugh. You weren't drunk. You were sweet. I loved you then,
and I've loved you since. I said yes when you proposed. We got
married. We had four kids and never fought. Wait. Maybe

that's too hard to believe. We did fight, but the sex was
great. Like it was when we fooled around in your parents'
basement, like when your dad came downstairs that one time
I almost gave in. I wasn't a prig. I didn't say no. I didn't insist

on waiting till later, till I got married, when I married that guy
who didn't care it was my first time. I didn't regret saving
myself, didn't divorce him later. I never tried to die. That
one guy? He was good to me. That other guy? He never cheated.

I'm so glad you were my first. *The Holy Grail* was funny: *Bring
out your dead. (I'm not dead!) It's just a flesh wound. We are the keepers
of the sacred word: Ni! Ni!* We were so young. Please, tell me a lie.
Tell me I said yes. Tell me I don't regret anything.

How to See the World: Hunger

When I first moved from Massachusetts to Indiana
I didn't know how to see the flat black fields stretching

all around me as anything but oceans of mud. It took
time to understand the lay of that land, its change

of season, and that newly turned soil as black as that
held every promise of richness, newness, nourishment,

food. I began to see it wasn't quite flat, that not all the
soil was so dark, that every rise or mounding, every

possible shade of brown, was a different kind of soil,
meant for a different kind of planting. But while it was

still new to me, when I felt the first pangs of homesick,
a wanting that has never left, I sat down on the edge of

one of those fields next to the man I knew by now I was
destined to marry (still blessedly ignorant I was destined,

too, to divorce him) and gestured hopelessly across
the landscape. *There's nothing to see here. Nothing to look at.*

The bleakness of what stretched around us matched
only the bleakness of what was inside. To his credit,

he didn't lash out or take my observation as insult. He
said one of the few things I ever thought wise or helpful.

I've been to the mountains, he said, *and I also thought there
was nothing to see. Those mountains were always in the way.*

How to See the World: Thirst

It's true that opposites attract, but also true
that things can just clash, like two puzzle

pieces that look like they should fit but don't;
they can't be forced. You've tried this, I know.

Once, I married a farmer. That's not what he
was when I met him, but it's where he ended

up and where I did, tied like a mule to that plow.
One night, we worked the fields long past time

to go in. We worked most nights that way, but
that night, in the morbid heat, we'd not brought

enough potable water. Potable: drinkable. God
knows we had a full tank of what would save

the tender plants twisting away from the brutal
sun. It's hard to say when we realized our own

supply would not be enough, hard to explain
how thirst turned suddenly to something it had

never been before: deadly. I saw for the first time
he was sorry, and for the first time in a long time

I could set my anger aside. All that mattered
was staying alive, truck too far away to get us

home to the trailer, fields too far from the road
for anyone to see us if we passed out. So, we

took turns with tiny sips of what we had left in
the single shared thermos. We wet our tongues

and traded, wet our tongues and traded again,
until something rose up inside me and I gulped it

all down. If someone was going to die, it wasn't
going to be me. (How many times have I fought

for my own life? Just that once?) When he saw
what I'd done, he nodded and looked pleased,

turned back to the tanker and finished the job
himself. We didn't die that day. Sun went down,

and we got home safely. We never stayed so late
again, but I can't say that was the lesson learned.

It was an open door, that desperate craving, that
honestly-dying-of-thirst. It's how it is sometimes,

how it is more often than not. There's a will to live
and a will to let live. They need not be in opposition.

Sleep

Some birds sleep on one leg, feathers fluffed
to expose the down, other leg pulled inside.

When some birds sleep, their toes flex into
an iron grip, keeping them solidly perched

on branch or wire or windowsill. Some birds
sleep with one eye open, brains split evenly into

alert-to-everything and dead-to-the-world,
like all but the lead bird in a V-formation.

Migration takes time, as anyone who's driven
the I-90 corridor east to west, state after state,

knows: eventually it's all a straight line, corn
lined up on either side of the road: *Turn on*

cruise control and take a nap, my sister said when
she'd come to visit me in Indiana. The Alpine

Swift, clocked half-awake two hundred days
at a time, knows that feeling, or maybe we've

come to know his, what it's like to just keep
going, no other choice but to drop and die.

Chin up, keep your eye on the sky. Let
yourself dream: Mountain, trees, the shore.

Fearful, Wanting, Full of Joy

I woke with only a remnant, my sister's face
close to mine, scared, vulnerable, grieving.
In dreams, every person is some version of
you. We call my sister Baby Lynda. My sister

is fifty years old. It's never too late to be born
again, to open ourselves to all that we are. In
the dream, I hold out my arms. *You've never
come to me for comfort before! Come!* I'm so happy

to hold her. She's so happy to be held. How
wonderful to be able to admit I'm all these
things: fearful, wanting, full of joy. Able to
comfort even my own sorrow. In dreams,

sometimes symbols are more than they seem,
catching on to the collective unconscious. Is
the child archetype all of us now: grieving and
wanting to be known? Asking the elders, those

guides who know where we're going, who've
been here before, to help? How lovely to think
they're ready and waiting: *Come to us, yes! We
know what to do! Come to us, exactly like this!*

FLYING

It was a few years back when this happened,
when a friend shared a photo of his daughter
in the pilot's seat of a small plane. She looked

grown and child-like at the same time, sweet,
awkward, smiling, crowded in this teeny-tiny
plane. And we oohed and ahhed and laughed.

Later, though, my feet felt the pedals below
them, steering that plane, steering one like it,
and a man sitting beside me (there was no man

beside me) smiled and said, *Yup, that's right,*
you're doing it now. I'm not helping at all. Then he
wasn't smiling, looked real serious instead

and said, *I'm taking over.* That's it. Maybe a
memory, maybe a dream. But I've never flown
a plane before; it can't be the first. I wasn't

asleep; it can't be the second. My feet, though,
my feet could feel those pedals, feel the plane
bank gently left now gently right *Just like that,*

that's right and who is this man beside me?
(There is no man beside me.) How is it possible
for me to know these pedals are a rudder

steering this plane? See, this is a story that's
hard to tell: I might have flown a plane, I might
have died trying. I've come to know since

another way or two I might have died: none
good. So, I think of the time or two I tried
to die and failed. That I told the doctors

meant god looked at me like a too-small fish
he had to throw back. Maybe it's not just
this life where I needed not to die too soon.

Maybe I died too soon once or twice before.
Maybe this time somebody somewhere is
saying *goddammit, she needs to see things through!*

Maybe it's me saying that. Or the kid flying
that plane. Or the guy who couldn't land it.
Anyway. This was all a few years back. I'm not

getting any younger, and it's common enough
for little local airports to offer free flying lessons
on Saturday afternoon—the one near me has

a banner up now. It just seems like something
you'd remember, flying a plane. Like something
more than one part of your body could recall.

WEIGHT

There are places where even I know
the air itself is heavy, and there are
places where the air is light. Once,

driving through a weightless place,
convinced I was levitating, I touched
the top of my head to see how much

space was left between me and the
roof, wondered briefly if "roof" could
be transcended. Could the car guide

itself if I continued to rise, last wisp
of hill fog lifting off the mountain? But
the car contained me, and a few miles

later I was solidly in my seat. I circled
back. I like the feel of rising. And I like
that I could prove that day, to no one

else but me, that places where the air
is light are real. It makes the weight of
other places easier to bear. I used to

think weight was something I carried:
shame, guilt, sorrow, something I
couldn't trace to its source. But when

air, heavy as all that, bears down, that's
the weight of so many people told so
many times they could not rise they just

stopped trying. And so we've stayed,
heavy. I can't explain places that never
bought in to the story of Can't. Won't.

Afraid to. Just Not Worthy. But I know
they're here, pockets of places where
people never believed much of anything

except the world is beautiful. Here's
a tree: perfect. Here's a cloud: perfect.
Tree and cloud never came to mean

Something Not Me. Somehow this little
patch of hill fog some folks call a haint
is just mountain being cloud, cloud

being mountain, neither one knowing
it was possible not to be the other.
That's what I mean by the light places,

pockets of the earth where people can
rise, where gravity's just different
somehow. It's nice. I hope you get to

go there, sometime. Or what I really
mean is, I hope you get to go back there,
that we all do, that all these heavy places

get to be light again. All it takes is to
stop believing what you were told or
even what I'm telling you now. You just

go off and see tree. See sky. See cloud.
See rain. See that hill fog. Just go off
thinking: That's beautiful. That's all me.

Flower Moon

Headed to bed late again—how it is I lose track
of time when the house goes dark is something
I can't explain—I slip past my sleeping husband

and into the bath, startled to see a light left on
where we've never had light before. The sink, it
turns out, the perfect, round, chipped-porcelain

sink, had captured the moonlight so it glowed
Spielberg-esque, I decided, stepping back to see
that the moon, high and round and perfect itself

was shining straight down into the basin, and she
was shining straight back up. Tell me there are no
miracles. Tell me moonlight can't speak, that

something as simple as this sink can't sing a fine
aria to what I saw so clearly in that moment had
inspired her very existence. Tell me the world

doesn't glow with miracles. I'll tell you this: last
night was not my first trip to Nirvana. Still I was
reluctant to be there again. But that tunnel of light

streaming through the bath, once I saw it for what
it was, charged the air so that even as I returned
to the fully dark bedroom, the air itself shimmered

with a light so beautiful it woke my husband who
reached out, thinking it was me. He rose up, placed
his open mouth on a hip bone I didn't know still

rose through this flesh. I'm not the girl I was once
when, lying flat, my belly formed a basin of its own,
waiting to be filled. Light begets light and recognizes

love, which rises, too, to meet it. Anything we've ever
named is nameless, each charged particle knows itself
only as part of every other one. That's what light is

and love: energy, life-force, holy existence. Meta,
Matter, Atman. Jah, baby. Ma. Me, you, the moon
and that sink. How love gives way to making love,

whether it should, is mystery itself. But my husband
slept beside me while I remembered stories of monks
walking at night under the moon. Circling a field

saying prayers for us all. It makes sense, now, that
monks and mystics retreat: cave, convent, desert,
abbey. This is a painful place. Sanguine grace, blood

of the sword, knowledge of all that was not, is not,
necessary. One need not suffer to see the moon,
to know it shines on every body of water: empty,

full, waiting. Ashes to ashes, dust to dust. *Remember*
that you are dust, we're told, and so we are. *To dust*
you shall return, it's true. This is a sacred promise:

soil and stardust are both the same. They saw each
other last night, sang a song that woke the man
in my bed. And who is he but every man who's ever

broken my heart. Who am I but one who knows
how to heal: him, you, me. Who am I but the moon
and basin, the one who sees, the one who sings back.

Earth Day Dream: Rumi

I'm home, it's lovely, and in the way of dreams,
everything is different: so many colors: pinks,
greens, baby blues, the softest yellows. Spring
finery. My partner, off camera—in the way of
dreams—has done a fine job. She wants me
to stay upstairs, but I must tend to the guests
I know are coming. I head down to the kitchen
and she's calling, *Don't go, don't go now.* But
this is a guest house. You're all on your way.

III.

Ant: Patience

My husband has not yet seen them, tiny sweet
bastards: sugar ants. But they're here: climbing

my arms while I sit on the sofa, mounting my toes
as I load the washer, scurrying the baseboards

while I make dinner. That they come to me means
I've something to learn. The lesson is nothing new:

Patience is a virtue, an art. The struggle for food,
for territory? That's war. Every year, I wrestle with

this: the scouts have been sent to find the food
their colony needs to survive. (This morning, it was

the dry, half-masticated food the cat had vomited
overnight. Who am I to judge the feasting?) Is there

any act more cruel than setting out traps for what
only wants to endure? Yet, if I had one, I would.

This year, I'm jealous of their journey. Perhaps that's
why they're drawn to me. I could choose to see it

as a taunting. But I think they mean to be kind. What
we crave is always a journey, they might be trying

to say. The strongest among us are crushed every
day. Yet here we are, creeping in droves. The needs

of the many are greater than the needs of the few.
Keep moving, keep moving. Stand very, very still.

Ode to Centipede (Or Maybe Elegy)

I know you must hold good strong medicine,
too. You would not come to me otherwise,

oh many-legged, feather-legged friend. I have
friended the vulture, the ant, the opossum.

I believe in and receive all of the lessons all
of you bring. Even in you, I see beauty, know

it in my flinch, my shudder, my turning away.
Twice you've come, twice I've let you go.

(Do you know what it is to restrain these mere
two legs, to keep them from running, from

stomping this laminate floor? Do you know
what it is for teeth to clench, to strangle a scream

while a husband sleeps upstairs? I hoped
you'd never return. But, oh, beautiful fluttering

legs! Oh, beauty too much for mine eyes!
I fling this veil, these delicate squares of paper,

draping you from these eyes, saving you
from this mine murderous, slippered heel. You

know I'm trying to save you? You know
that I know every terrible beauty from which

we turn away brings us an unavoidable truth,
the lesson we most need to learn? Let's call this

third arrival a reckoning. You were nearly
invisible in this silver, stainless-steel sink. I nearly

rinsed you down the drain. It seems my out,
oh creature—is my lesson this fear? This guilt?

This awe for all you can do? Will you return
in my nightmares, crawling up out of this pipe?

Will you actually crawl out of this pipe? Is is
my destination to search for you always, even

after you're gone? I've now come fully undone.
You are not squashed, my pretty, there's that. I

shall let myself believe you can save yourself,
somewhere down this drain. O centipede, is that

the lesson? We save ourselves a hundred times,
a thousand. Is the use of your legs this counting?

Oh, that I might be sorry to see you go. O
my beautiful teacher, my terrible, terrible friend.

Math

When a friend in Pago Pago, seven time zones away,
tells me he sends his love, I wonder: is it today there

or is it tomorrow? Is this a gift I'm expecting or one
I need only remember? Thirty years ago, we met in

Mississippi. I headed north to Ohio, he made his way
to American Samoa. I ask him if it's still Monday there;

he replies by sending a map. We live in an age of endless
numerical models. Pandemics accentuate the math. Yes,

he says finally, it's Monday. But cross the International
Date Line, it's Tuesday. Cross the islands here, he laughs,

and you can celebrate a birthday twice in two days. Oh,
we are born and born again. Witness abounds—are we

charting it still? My friend, born to play blues across
fields of cotton, has grown to surf the radio waves

keeping every island signaling sound and song. The
Samoan archipelago, he tells me, is split politically. But

culturally we are one. Ah, sweet Jo. I always had trouble
with algebra. X is a concept I just couldn't fathom. And

geometry...well, it goggles the mind. Perhaps there's
more than math at stake, but surely you're proving this:

what's unknown is only the invisible thread that ties us
all together. North and South, cotton and corn, heartland

to island to island. Time is an artificial construct. That's
always been clear. But so is separation. Sunsets melt so

easily to Sunrise: birthday to birthday, death to glorious
rebirth. The world is round; it's a circle. We live in an age

of flattening curves. Long ago, I was your teacher. Today
the lesson is yours. You said you see time as a prism. I said

I'd have to agree. Let's see light as a rainbow, a curve that
will never unbend. Every stripe is time, every color a mile.

When we meet in the middle, we'll capture the sun and
blow all our kisses to faraway stars. The number of stars is

countless, but together we've solved the unknown. Time
is one axis, space is another. X? That's always been love.

Wheel

My friend who found the opossum
in her garage keeps a trapped, wild
mouse in a cage. Hector doesn't like
her, she says, but seems quite happy

otherwise. His favorite time to play
on his wheel is while she conducts
meetings online. Hector has been
on my mind all day: we know now

what it's like to wonder how we
came to be where we are, to run
toward the ever-dimming memory
of what life was like before: scents

on the wind, sun burning on your back,
what it was like to chew through
a wall. As long as these seeds are here,
cotton balls, this wheel, it's just

as well really to put a nicer spin on
things, settle into comfortable routine
with the one you find yourself with.
There are worse things, I imagine Hector

chants on his wheel, tidy little cadence
call to help him believe he's moving
forward. Much worse things. There
are worse things than living like this.

Torpor

From dusk till dawn the Poorwill calls
its name: *poor-will poor-will poor-will*

till, come winter, even he seems tired
of hearing himself talk. Concealed in

a pile of rocks, he slows his breathing,
slows his heartbeat, slowly lowers his

body temperature, and... stays there.
Weeks. Months. Till it's warm again.

Till he feels like calling his name once
more: *poor-will, poor-will poor-will.* Do

you see me here? *Do-you?* Do you care?
Do you? *Poor-will poor-will poor-will.*

Justice

Two herons were building a nest. The first one
stretched his slender neck toward the second,

who delivered the long, slim, broken branches
that would fashion their home. I've always said it:

even so beautiful, birds can be cruel. The sticks
he brought her, he stole. The calls that filled the air

came from herons whose homes were being
destroyed. I'll say it again: birds rival even us

for what they do. Loving this world so much
they steal for their own survival. Keening grief

to the wind they think will hear. Believing that
someone somewhere will understand, will answer.

What's Not in Our Nature

Still-blind honeyguide chicks,
newly hatched from their shells,
use perfectly pointed beaks to
puncture any eggs still left in
the nest. Carnivorous shrikes
impale their prey on any spike
they can find. The whole world
watched on a livestream cam
while a Pittsburgh peregrine
falcon fed one dead hatchling
to one that survived. I mean,
we'd rather not know the ways
of the wild, where our hungry
hearts might lead. We see a bird
soar and call it free, fight for
the right to live the same way
knowing peace means nothing
to parasite, that might, on its own,
never yields to mercy. We see
ourselves as songbirds only, but
given the hunger, given the cause,
given our driving fear, we wake
up singing in the morning sun
what just doesn't jibe with the
nightly news. It helps not to turn
away from the world, to see with
grace these gifts we're given:
the will to live, this want to rise.

Routine

In March, sea-ice slowly surrounds
Antarctica so ships cannot break

through. Dark, cold, rife with storm,
this is where the emperor penguins

begin their breeding, males offering
an ecstatic display, couples raising

their heads and necks together in
perfect, mirrored form. They bow,

each to the other, hold pose as if
assuaging doubt or guilt, copulate

and produce the single, pale green,
pear-shaped egg she rolls onto his

feet. For sixty-five days, he incubates
the egg under a fold of skin while she

returns to the sea to feed. He fasts
and tries not to freeze as the fierce

darkness swirls in storms around him
for weeks. Huddled by the hundreds,

backs to the wind, the male emperor
penguins keep each other warm while

they waste away. Their body weight
drops by half before the thick-shelled

egg beneath them begins to hatch.
It can take three days, just this, chick

working its way out of the egg's thick
shell. When they do, their fathers feed

them the curd-like crop-milk meant to
sustain them till their mothers return.

The emperor penguin breeding process
has taken them through April, May,

June, and now July, when the females
return, if they return—sea, too, a cruel

mistress. Can you imagine the sound
of his call as she hauls herself, fat and

fit for the rest of the brooding, back
up onto the ice? It's what she follows

to find him, starving, still reluctant to
leave. Staying in place, even in these

conditions, has become routine. What
has hatched while waiting, tender and

hungry now, too, opens its mouth for
what its mother has fed on. It takes

time for the male to return comfortably
to the sea. Even then, he comes back

again and again, taking turns with his
mate, brooding and foraging, brooding

and foraging, until August turns to
September, September to November,

and the chicks molt into full plumage
finally feeding themselves. It's summer

now. Winter lasted a long, long time.
It's seems no wonder, really, that the

Emperor Penguins, faithful as they are
to the process, don't mate for life. Free

from the sea-ice, they dive deep into
open waters, surfacing only to breathe.

Thrush

One day, walking along a rural highway,
I saw a turtle up ahead in full silhouette:
the long stretch of her neck, lovely curve

of her shell. I marveled at her eagerness
to cross the road, neck so curiously long
I squinted into my approach, gradually

seeing it wasn't a turtle's neck at all, but
the tail of a fallen bird. Close enough
now to kneel carefully beside the hermit

thrush barely bigger than the palm of my
hand, I studied him closely to believe he
really was dead. One leg stretched absurdly

straight and long, foot and toes perfectly
en pointe. I couldn't see his other leg till I
turned him over, saw it curled up tightly

against his body on the other side. Each eye
a small black crater, I guessed he'd been
there a pretty good while. I wanted to be

on my way, but meeting the thrush had
thrown me off my game. I wanted to be
done with telling this story, any story,

wanted Earth and Sky to tell me they had
no more gifts to give, and here was this
turtle become bird before me, symbol of

earth turned to spirit of death. I turned to
the wind and howled. Have at me! I cried.
What else ya got? I can take it! I opened my

arms to all of it and heard the rumble of
a car, heard it before it appeared, older
model, beat up, non-descript, white sedan.

Of course, it was white, O Mechanical Spirit
of Henry Ford! O Spirit of Dodge and
Chrysler! O Toyota! O Honda! O Kia Soul!

I considered standing my ground in the
center of the road, shaking my fist at
the car. But truly—or at least, after only

a moment's hesitation—I took no offense
at the driver's intrusion. This is how the
world works. We impose ourselves on each

other in all kinds of ways. I let the car pass,
bowed my head as it whipped by. Clearly
the car had little interest in me or in this bird.

We live, we die, we rise again! I shouted to the
blue air all around me. But then I stopped,
cocked my ear, and listened. *Yes*, I nodded.

Yes. It's true: sometimes we just disappear.
It's important, I think, or helpful at least, to
see all the world, everything that happens

to us, as metaphor while acknowledging
at the same time it simply is what it is. I
found a bird dead in the road. Time ebbs,

and it flows. The world is a terrible, beautiful
place where those not with us are with us
all the time. All of us not dead are dying,
all of us are spirits waiting to be found.

IV.

How to See the World: Fire

Once, the first husband and I—Yankee and a
Yankee's Yankee—living in a trailer in a field

at the mouth of the Delta, decided to throw
a party in the yard. What I remember about

Mississippi is mostly the heat, but it must
have cooled off long enough for us to us to

feel like we needed a fire. I was always up
for adventure back then, had moved from

Massachusetts to Indiana, Florida to Alabama
to Mississippi. I worked as sign-painter, carnie,

ice cream maker, obit writer, educator. I was
always happy, despite the sadness, some

sorrow I could never figure out. Anyway, we
had this party, this fire, and all these people

who were all so happy, too, and so sad. And
long-haired Joe said, *Hey, y'all know how to*

beat a fire, right? Anybody got a big enough
stick? When we found a tree branch big enough,

he taught us how to do it, how to beat that
fire, lifting the big stick over his head and

bringing it down again hard so sparks flew
everywhere: fireworks. An orange-embered

explosion of joy. *Go on and try it,* he said to me.
I declined, but he told me again to go on. So

I swung that stick and swung it again, beating
the fire till sparks raged all around us, till

long-haired Joe had to pull me away: *That's*
enough. The party wrapped up, guests collecting

beer cans and crock pots, calling out goodbyes.
The fire went out, everywhere except inside me.

That one's always lit now. And you'd best believe
I beat it, too, whenever I feel a party coming on.

I beat it just like Joe taught me: lifting the weight
of what I carry, bringing it down, hard, to burn.

Tension

Today was not a test. When the sirens started
wailing, I was so deep in focused concentration

I almost didn't notice. Not till I saw the light
wasn't right, or the time, and my brain broke

through the task at hand and I thought to ask
what time it was, what day it was, and I still

couldn't make sense how the county got things
so wrong. The siren cycled *LOUD and then soft,*

LOUD and then soft, LOUD and then soft till
my heart picked up the rhythm thinking it would

burst. Here, three minutes of siren are followed
by seven minutes of silence where you try to

convince yourself danger has passed. What
you just heard still rings in your ear, memory

maybe. Premonition? What you don't hear
becomes what you pray for: something to tell

you what to do. Stay still or run for your life.
All that's left is to wait, tension building in a way

that's hard to explain, like the air itself knows
something needs to break through somewhere.

I hear the sky burst... rain, relief... and see a text
from my daughter telling me baby's first tooth

just broke through the gums. Christ, synchronicity.
She's been teething for weeks, meltdown after

meltdown, keeping everyone awake and begging
for mercy. Mercy comes like a storm sometimes,

prayers answered in ways we never would have
asked, trees uprooted, somebody's barn ripped

to the ground. Nobody killed, this time. Next text
is a photo of baby sleeping soundly, no way of

knowing she'll suffer more storms than this one.
No care in the world another is already brewing.

Beast

Strange portal, this phone in my hand.
I'm suddenly watching a horse in labor,

terror in her eyes, gray-haired farmer
behind her, still-bagged hooves in his

hands. His wife holds the mare's head,
son stands by waiting to be told what

to do, daughter films it all on her phone.
First birth, mare too tight, foal too big,

the blue-white bag farmer holds on to
disappears back inside. I didn't ask for

this. From the looks of things, the mare
didn't either. Yet here we both are, and

I'll be damned if I'll leave this heaving
beast or what's inside her fighting to get

out. Or this farmer still holding on to a
pair of suddenly long legs, good lord!

Horse totem tells us how we might tame
our own wild energy, how we might ride

wind freely. Here, horse still tethered to
horse, foal bursting free from the mare?

Energy begets energy, opposite of paired
opposites, poem begets poem, torn from

us line by line. The family, still in their pj's,
have all changed places, all but the dad

helped now by wife now holding this head,
this ever-elongating new body, while son

holds the phone, daughter tells mare in a
soothing tone what a fine job she's doing.

I almost believe her. When the foal fully
born lies naked on its own, they turn horse

around, lead her to see what's she's done.
Horse stares, fully unable to comprehend

anything, and the daughter soothes and
soothes and leads her nose down to what

she still wants nothing to do with. Farmer
dad, familiar with the process, concerned

and bemused and still so patient, reaches
to drag the foal to a cleaner patch of straw.

Daughter leads horse over, *soothesoothe*
soothe, guides her nose down, and tongue

flicks out, flared nostrils sniff, uncertain
still. It takes time for mare to see this

not-yet-wild horse spirit for what it is:
part of her. Heart unbound. Spirit made

flesh. When her tongue remembers what
it's supposed to do, lick and taste and

clean, the family backs slowly away,
clearing the stall. Horse and new-horse

know what to do. This was supposed
to happen, I eventually learn. The mare

really was too tight. The foal really was
unfathomably long. They really did need

help from someone who'd seen it before,
who knew how to coax new life in, how

to teach the beast so reluctant to let go
that everything could be okay. How nice

of the family to turn off their phone once
what they'd witnessed was normal again

and sweet, just that one last glimpse of
mother and child so tender together. We

need not see so much of that. We know
how things are supposed to be when all

goes right with the world. What we're not
so good at, what we need to learn, is how

to witness pain, see struggle, see even
this wild terror, this difficult birthing,

see what comes of it, see what, once
fathomed, we can learn how to love.

Deluge: Edenville Dam

Song sparrow sings
of what she saw. What she didn't.
Field and flood. Forewarning.

Black-capped chickadee
steals black oil seeds,
hammers them against her branch:
we told you! we told you!

Starlings only murmur
pulsing shadows pulsing
beautifully pulsing shadows dark
pulsing.

Blue jays screech
as blue jays do, annoyed.
Blue jays screech
as blue jays do, annoyed.

Robins weep their way through,
springtime manic:
cheer up! cheer up!
cheerily! cheerily!
cheer up! cheer up!
cheerily! cheerily!

Starlings just keep murmuring
pulsing shadows pulsing
dark shadows beautifully pulsing
dark shadows drowning
pulsing.

Lexicon of the Void: A Poem in Two Parts

void / void/ adj. 1 (especially of a contract or agreement) not valid or legally binding. 2 (void of) free from: lacking: the tundra is seemingly void of life. 3 completely empty.
n. a completely empty space.
v. 1 declare that something is not valid or legally binding. 2 to discharge or to drain away water, gases, waste matter, etc.

I. Synonym

Invalid, null, nullified, cancelled.
Useless, worthless, nugatory, expired.
Terminated.
Architecture of the barren womb. (see: human, female.
    see also: planet, earth)
Relationship of the orphan to the mother he/ she/ they
    has lost. (see: ache. see also: archipelago of longing)
Relationship of the mother to the child he/ she/ they
    has lost. (see torn. see also: wrench, wring, dislocate.
    see also: n. desert. consider: flood, fire, etc.)

Revoked, rescinded, abolished, discontinued.
Empty, emptied, vacant, blank, bare.
Free from, lacking.
Unoccupied, uninhabited. Desolate. (see pandemic,
    streets therein.)
Devoid of, vacant of, bereft of. Denuded.
Without.
Wanting.

Gap, space, vacuum, lacuna, hole. (see: distance of six feet,
    pandemic)
Cavity, chasm, abyss. (see: separation. see also: restrictions
    from touch.)
Gulf, pit, hiatus, emptiness. (see: grief. see: despair. see:
    memory. see also: the disconnect of artificial respiratory
    devices)
Nothingness. Blank.
Vacancy, vacuity, oblivion.

II. Antonymn

Valid, sound, supportable, sustainable.
Legally acceptable, bona fide, official.
Legitimate. Licit.
Ratify. (see: approve, sanction, accept, affirm, uphold.)
Full. (see: heart, hearts, etc. see also: reunion. see also:
flora and fauna of a healing planet)
Occupied. (see: architecture of the post pandemic. see
also: limitations thereof. see: pandemic, streets therein.
see also: torn, ache, grief, etc.)
Reclaimed, redeemed.
Reconditioned, rehabilitated, repeopled.

Brimming, bulging, bursting, chock-full.
Saturated, stuffed, swarming.
Teeming, thick, thronging. (see: choke. see also:
lessons we've learned, consideration thereof.)
Furnished, provided, supplied.
Completeness. Fullness.
Replete.

Brave: Titan Arum

Tonight I watch the corpse flower
on a YouTube live feed; it's getting
ready to bloom. The lights are low

in the Barnard College greenhouse,
the feed vibrates grainy grayscale
lush, the bulbous stalk is centered

in a landscape you can call serene.
Four weeks ago, it broke dormancy
rising like a thumb through the soil.

Two weeks later, it was ten inches tall.
It was five-foot-two this morning and
now stands most certainly taller than

me. The cataphylls are off (earlier, I
looked up "cataphyll") exposing the
frilled spathe (I looked that up too).

Think: an ear of corn, upright, and
you've shucked one layer of leaves.
Imagine a burgundy phallus wearing

asymmetrical hip-hugging pleats,
chartreuse green. Think beautiful.
Think horticultural drag queen. Think

male and female simultaneity. The plant
is called Berani: Brave. This momentous
occasion took ten years. The bloom,

when it happens, lasts twenty-four
hours. Spathe will open like a frilly
inverted parasol, the temperature

will rise, spadix will offer up the stank
signaling it's time for pollinating
insects to do their duty. I'm not sure

yet how that will work. I'm willing to
wait. These days I don't look too far
ahead. One more friend passed away

this morning. Another friend's daughter
still can't speak—she might never be
able to talk again. The whole world

watched one man kneel on another
man's neck; I'm not made to understand
prayer like that. This corpse flower,

endangered itself, chose this moment
to raise itself up and bloom. I'm willing
to witness the miracle. I won't turn away.

Dirge

o bella ciao, bella ciao,
bella ciao, ciao, ciao

In between abominations, I ponder
these two things: the corpse plant
blooming and the eagle found dead

in a lake, floating face down. Dead
man's float, we used to call it, wings
useless at his sides, stabbed through

the heart by a loon. That damn plant,
so big, so beautiful, smelling so foul,
and the dead loon chick that made

his mother strike. Death is in the air,
cry of the loon, carrion flower calling
beetles and flesh flies. This is not news:

eagle deserved to die. This is dirge
for the chick. For his mother. For all
that looms, stinking now of promise.

The Detail Left Out

I.
When his uncle sent the big Crane-demon
to kill him, Krishna was so very young the
monster swallowed him whole. Once inside,
he burned with a light so bright it set fire
to demon's mouth. Krishna was vomited
out unharmed, and the demon died.

II.
Every god has a story of burning: Ra and Oya.
Agni, Fiji, Vulcan. The bright red bush who
called to Moses. Good and evil, always paired,
create the complicated story of divine energy.

III.
The crimson-crowned Indian sarus crane,
world's tallest flying bird, mates for life.
Losing that mate, it starves itself to death.
What's left when the crane is gone, grief
nothing now but hollow bone? The greater
good, perhaps. Yearning its own forging.

IV.
Indian sarus cranes mate in the rainy season,
trumpet loudly from a coiled trachea, engage
in spectacular display of calling and posturing.
They raise their young in an island nest
completely unconcealed. What more godly
creature than this? Still: crow, dingo, kite.

V.
Such is the power of Krishna. The burning
bush was left unharmed. Is the lesson really
that only good prevails, or can we call struggle
itself a saving? Consider the crane. Study
their spectacular display. Remember that
separated, there is only the starving.

Testament: Old, New

When the waters began to recede, Noah released both
Raven and Dove. Which returned and how many times

depends on who you read. Raven, released, may have
refused to return. Forty days trapped in a cage, flight

seems a rational response. Who returns to their captor?
Consider this raven, whom the lord has fed, who suffers

as symbol of darkness and light. Liberated, what's left
for him on a ship that wants only a harbor? It's hollow

bone that allows each bird its flight. Consider the raven
rising, rising. Consider: why would the dove return?

Windows

I walked my house window to window
today, following and FaceTiming the
masked arborist in my yard. *Root rot,*
he says: the arborvitae gone brown. *Dead,*

eight double-planted spruce. *Fungus,*
weeping cherry out front. Endless obituary
of dead and about-to-die. It's not all bad
news: what can be trimmed, what will

sprout back into "manageable." It's a litany,
really, of the untended, unmanaged, the
left-too-long unfed. Litany, too, of family
illness, sick children, we'll-put-money-aside,

other-things-need-fixing-first. Graduations,
birthdays, car wrecks, cancer. Stroke. Anxiety,
grief, depression, recovery, each new wave
of all of the above. I point to the robins' nest

that he can't see, he tells me how the pear
tree can fruit within our reach. There's life
out there, and possibility. A less cramped
and crowded view of the world. What's lost,

we agree, makes way for what will be healthy
new growth. Too used to tangle and decay,
squirrels leaping merrily on the roof, sparrows
in the gutters, we've let the too-wild world

come too close while still keeping distance
from what, maybe, was only asking for help.
The brightest cardinal I'd ever seen jumped
in front of me, turned to see if I was paying

attention. The world needs a heavy hand
sometimes, it seems he said. Some shit just
has to go. I startled at the yellow of his beak,
the flame of his life. What was I to do but listen?

Ecclesiastes

Merest breath, said Qohelet, merest breath. All is mere breath.
—Qohelet (Ecclesiastes) 1:2, trans. Robert Alter

I measure time in the curl of my husband's hair at the nape
of his neck, the number of times I've trimmed my toenails.
I sleep when sleep comes, every dream a palimpsest.

The hyacinth are gone; we're heavy with hydrangeas now.
A volunteer maple grows where the dogwood died. What
I mean to say is, life goes on, if not how we'd planned.

When did what we plan ever fall into place? Who did it help,
and how many suffered instead? They say the gods laugh.
Maybe. Have you heard hyena, the wind before a storm,

kookaburra? I say we might be the source of the blue jay's
irritation: *Get on with it, then, what you feel you must do. Quit*
wasting my time. There's good in the world and bad.

We've all been both of those. There are forces at work
all around us. Rise up for what you believe in: the sun,
the moon, the glaciers melting. Ancestors calling our names.

These are worthy endeavors. Rest when body says rest—
that's worthy, too. The groceries that took two weeks
to arrive now land on the porch in hours. This is not

convenience. We adjust too easily to what technology tells us
to do. We're eating the onions that grew from the scraps
I planted. And that maple seedling didn't sprout exactly

where it is now. I hated the dogwood and wasn't sorry
it died. It was planted by someone I'm glad is gone, sorry
only for what she took with her. She planted the dogwood

in fury and fear; it never stood a chance. The roots did not
dig in—why would they? And my misguided sorrow was
never any help. We mourned its death the way so many do:

by keeping ourselves busy. We called it moving on. Who
moves on from death? Only those who take the time to
grieve. What we lost nearly always seems like something

we can't replace. For a good long time, that part of the yard
stayed empty while other parts grew wild. But I nurtured
what I could. I made mistakes, tearing out what I thought

were weeds: bee balm, rose campion. That was anger, too,
and fear, for the prickly sow thistle landing me in urgent care
too many times to count. Good god, the ways that we lash out.

Years passed. A baby was born in crisis. A father died in crisis.
These are things that slow us down—or should. But crisis
has a way of begetting only crisis. Am I sorry the world is

standing still? Sorry there's nothing left to look at but
ourselves? I'm not. The perennials rose again and again till
I recognized what they were. I found the maple seedling,

put it where the dogwood died. Every day, I kneel beside it,
talk to it and listen. Every day, I tell the tree it's loved, out loud,
so I can hear the words. I make my hands touch the earth so

she feels nurtured too. The roots are reaching down. Earth is
taking hold. This is how to see the world; the way it's always
been. This is how to love the world, the way it's always been.

How to See the World: Breath

I know you are there, little anger, my
old friend. Breathe—I am taking care
of you now.
—Thich Nhat Hanh

It takes more than lungs to breathe.
It takes head and neck and thoracic
cavity...can you feel the pelvis softly

pivot? Wind is breath—air sweeping
through the tops of trees and singing
past the plains—so let's ask those who

chart the jet stream, arborists and
botanists, all the fire spotters keeping
watch from parkland towers, what

it is that keeps us going, how it is
we're all connected. Ask blues man,
jazz singer, every opera diva, ask any

trumpet player how breath becomes
our instrument. Ask bullet blasting
through why it is that blood flows red.

Ask the birds why every new-born
baby pushed from the womb cries out.
Every breath is a battle cry, refusing

to retreat. (See that brand-new baby
reaching for the light? See his tiny fist,
wanting, too, to live?) Source is not

she who bore us. Source is she who
feeds, she from whom all waters
flow. Listen, bad smells tell us what

we should all avoid. Good smells say
come closer. Sometimes one gives way
to another. Remember the titan arum?

Corpse plant, carrion flower? Even
she smells sweet as pumpkin once
her work is done. I'm prone, myself,

to hyperventilation, my body swoons
from too much breath too fast. I've
learned to savor each inhale, to take

things in and let them go. This is how
we see the world: fire, flood, famine.
This is what it gives: anger, tears,

the taste for something more. Sit with
these; it makes us stronger. Sit with
these, it makes us wiser. Sit where

you can't see; see how you still can.
Feel the world fill your lungs. Hold it
near your heart. Mother Earth has

birthed us, new-born babies wailing.
Let your breath go slowly, slowly.
See how breath can move the world.

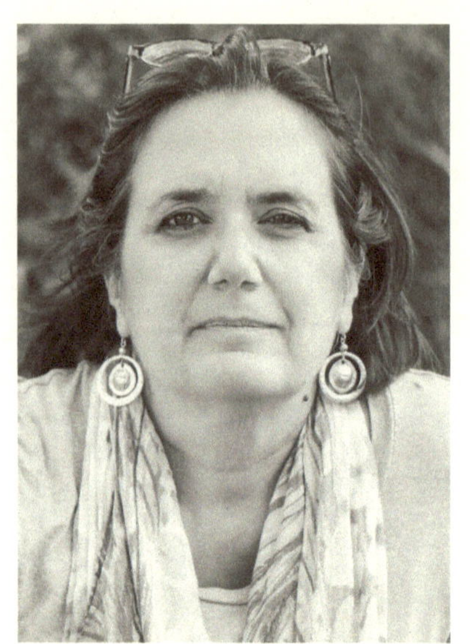

About the Author

Paula J. Lambert, a native of Massachusetts and graduate of Butera School of Art in Boston, worked as a sign painter in Indiana, Florida, and Alabama before earning her BA and MA degrees from the University of Alabama at Birmingham. She also worked briefly as an ice cream maker, carnie, and obituary writer. She went on to earn her MFA degree from Bowling Green State University, teaching composition and creative writing at the college level for a total of twenty years in Alabama, Mississippi, and Ohio.

Lambert has published several collections of poetry. Her most recent work has focused on the anatomy of birds: by digging deep into their bones, beaks, and feathers, she has found her way to issues both deeply personal and broadly political. She has been recipient of two Ohio Arts Council Individual Excellence Awards and two Greater Columbus Arts Council Artist in the Community Resource Grants. She has twice been a fellow of the Virginia Center for Creative Arts.

She owns and operates Full/Crescent Press, a small publisher of poetry books and broadsides. Through this she has founded and supported numerous public readings and festivals supporting the intersection of poetry and science, including the annual Sun & Moon Poetry Festival. She lives in Columbus with her husband Dr. Michael Perkins, a philosopher and technologist.

Books by Bottom Dog Press
Working Lives Series

Yeoman's Work: Poems, by Garrett Stack, 90 pgs, $16

Appalachian Writing Series

Mama's Song, by P. Shaun Neal, 238 pgs, $18
Fissures and Other Stories, by Timothy Dodd, 152 pgs, $18
Old Brown, by Craig Paulenich, 92 pgs, $16
A Wounded Snake: A Novel, by Joseph G. Anthony, 262 pgs, $18
Brown Bottle: A Novel, by Sheldon Lee Compton, 162 pgs, $18
A Small Room with Trouble on My Mind,
by Michael Henson, 164 pgs, $18
Drone String: Poems, by Sherry Cook Stanforth, 92 pgs, $16
Voices from the Appalachian Coalfields, by Mike and Ruth Yarrow,
Photos by Douglas Yarrow, 152 pgs, $17
Wanted: Good Family, by Joseph G. Anthony, 212 pgs, $18
Sky Under the Roof: Poems, by Hilda Downer, 126 pgs, $16
Green-Silver and Silent: Poems, by Marc Harshman, 90 pgs, $16
The Homegoing: A Novel, by Michael Olin-Hitt, 180 pgs, $18
*She Who Is Like a Mare: Poems of Mary Breckinridge
and the Frontier Nursing Service*, by Karen Kotrba, 96 pgs, $16
Smoke: Poems, by Jeanne Bryner, 96 pgs, $16
Broken Collar: A Novel, by Ron Mitchell, 234 pgs, $18
The Pattern Maker's Daughter: Poems,
by Sandee Gertz Umbach, 90 pgs, $16
The Free Farm: A Novel, by Larry Smith, 306 pgs, $18
Sinners of Sanction County: Stories,
by Charles Dodd White, 160 pgs, $17
Learning How: Stories, Yarns & Tales, by Richard Hague, $18
The Long River Home: A Novel, by Larry Smith,
230 pgs, cloth $22; paper $16
Eclipse: Stories, by Jeanne Bryner, 150 pgs, $16

Appalachian Writing Series Anthologies

Unbroken Circle: Stories of Cultural Diversity in the South,
Eds. Julia Watts and Larry Smith, 194 pgs, $18
Appalachia Now: Short Stories of Contemporary Appalachia,
Eds. Charles Dodd White and Larry Smith, 178 pgs, $18
Degrees of Elevation: Short Stories of Contemporary Appalachia,
Eds. Charles Dodd White and Page Seay, 186 pgs, $18

Free Shipping.

Books by Bottom Dog Press
Harmony Series

How to See the World, by Paula J. Lambert, 94 pgs, $16
Quilt Life, by Cindy Bosley, 108 pgs, $16
Family Portrait with Scythe, by James Owens, 114 pgs, $16
The Pears: Poems, by Larry Smith, 66 pgs, $15
Without a Plea, by Jeff Gundy, 96 pgs, $16
Taking a Walk in My Animal Hat, by Charlene Fix, 90 pgs, $16
Earnest Occupations, by Richard Hague, 200 pgs, $18
Pieces: A Composite Novel, by Mary Ann McGuigan, 250 pgs, $18
Crows in the Jukebox: Poems, by Mike James, 106 pgs, $16
Portrait of the Artist as a Bingo Worker: A Memoir,
by Lori Jakiela, 216 pgs, $18
The Thick of Thin: A Memoir, by Larry Smith, 238 pgs, $18
Cold Air Return: A Novel, by Patrick Lawrence O'Keeffe, 390 pgs, $20
Flesh and Stones: A Memoir, by Jan Shoemaker, 176 pgs, $18
Waiting to Begin: A Memoir, by Patricia O'Donnell, 166 pgs, $18
And Waking: Poems, by Kevin Casey, 80 pgs, $16
Both Shoes Off: Poems, by Jeanne Bryner, 112 pgs, $16
Abandoned Homeland: Poems, by Jeff Gundy, 96 pgs, $16
Stolen Child: A Novel, by Suzanne Kelly, 338 pgs, $18
The Canary: A Novel, by Michael Loyd Gray, 196 pgs, $18
On the Flyleaf: Poems, by Herbert Woodward Martin, 106 pgs, $16
The Harmonist at Nightfall: Poems of Indiana, by Shari Wagner, 114 pgs, $16
Painting Bridges: A Novel, by Patricia Averbach, 234 pgs, $18
Ariadne & Other Poems, by Ingrid Swanberg, 120 pgs, $16
The Search for the Reason Why: New and Selected Poems, by Tom Kryss, 192 pgs, $16
Kenneth Patchen: Rebel Poet in America, by Larry Smith,
Revised 2nd Edition, 326 pgs, Cloth $28
Selected Correspondence of Kenneth Patchen,
Edited with introduction by Allen Frost, Paper $18/ Cloth $28
Awash with Roses: Collected Love Poems of Kenneth Patchen,
Eds. Laura Smith and Larry Smith with introduction by Larry Smith, 200 pgs, $16
Breathing the West: Great Basin Poems, by Liane Ellison Norman, 96 pgs, $16
Maggot: A Novel, by Robert Flanagan, 262 pgs, $18
American Poet: A Novel, by Jeff Vande Zande, 200 pgs, $18
The Way-Back Room: Memoir of a Detroit Childhood,
by Mary Minock, 216 pgs, $18

Bottom Dog Press, Inc.

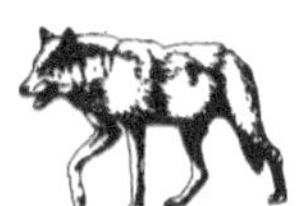

P.O. Box 425 /Huron, Ohio 44839
HTTP://SMITHDOCS.NET

www.ingramcontent.com/pod-product-compliance
Lightning Source LLC
LaVergne TN
LVHW051015080826
845145LV00009B/2642

* 9 7 8 1 9 4 7 5 0 4 2 3 3 *